THE MONSTERS IN MY HEAD

SABRINA RG RAVEN

The Monsters In My Head

Copyright © 2019
Sabrina RG Raven

All rights reserved. No part of this publication may be reproduced, stored in a retrieval system or transmitted in any form or by any means, electronic, mechanical, photocopying, recording or otherwise, without the prior written permission of the publisher

The information, views, opinions and visuals expressed in this publication are solely those of the author(s) and do not reflect those of the publisher. The publisher disclaims any liabilities or responsibilities whatsoever for any damages, libel or liabilities arising directly or indirectly from the contents of this publication.

Published by Ouroborus Book Services
www.ouroborusbooks.com

Art by Sabrina RG Raven
www.sabrinargraven.com

The Monsters in My Head

Sabrina RG Raven

As a child I was scared,
Of the monsters under my bed.
Then I grew up to fear,
The monsters in my head.

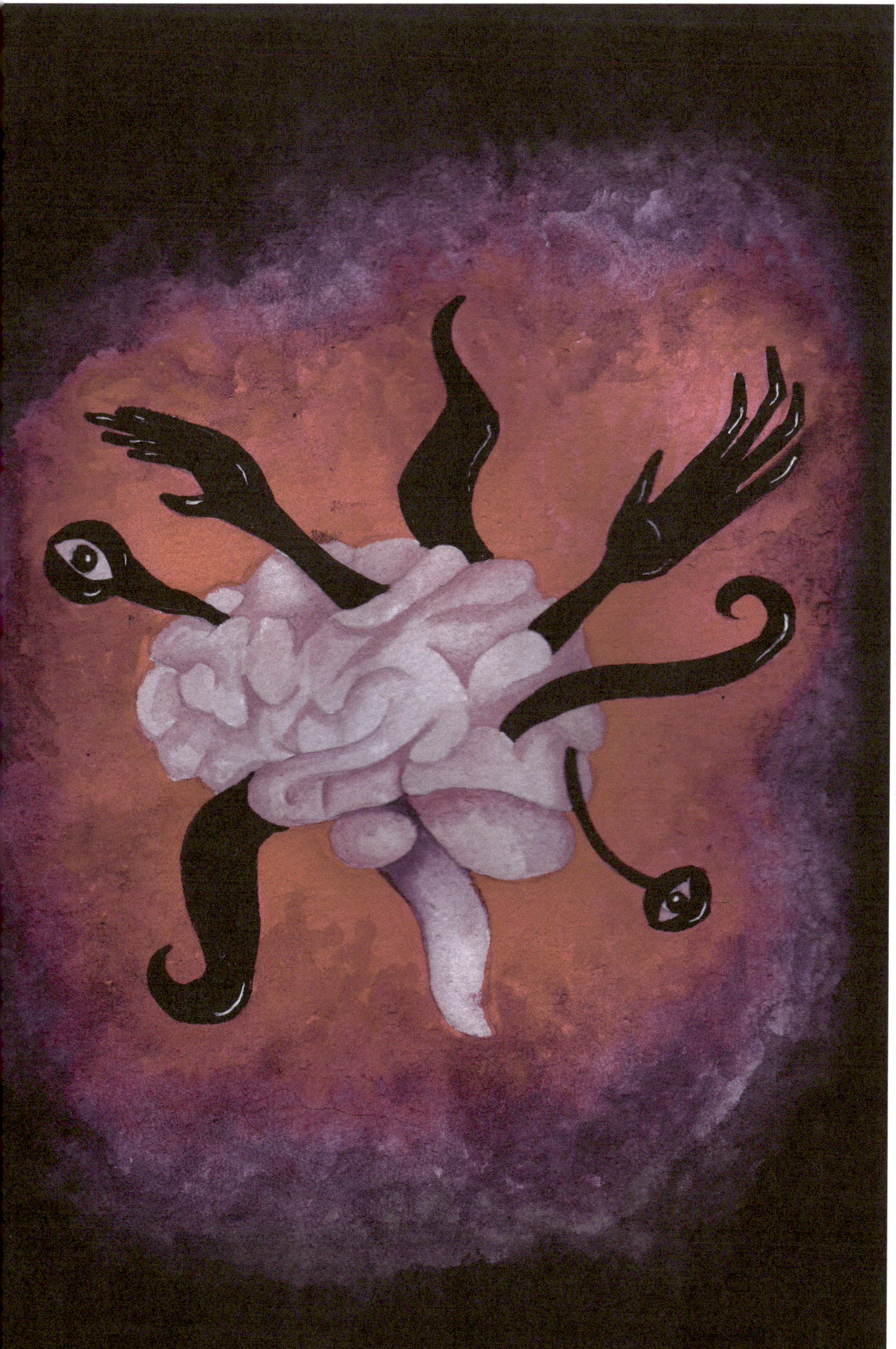

I CAN FEEL IT PRESSING DOWN,
CRUSHING ME FROM ABOVE.
IT IS TAKING ALL MY FEELINGS.
IT IS TAKING ALL MY LOVE.

I can feel its hungry eyes,
Reaching out to devour.
Its eating me up inside,
Gobbling up my power.

It takes its form to push me,
I try to hold the scraps.
Putting pieces in order,
Fighting memory lapse.

I feel so numb and hollow,
Emptiness devours me.
I hurt myself to feel,
Anything to make me free.

I reach out, got no choice,
Solid dark feels secure.
Darkness drips over me,
Depression hard and sure.

Can't eat, can't sleep.
Shaking like a leaf.
Near tears, full of fears.
Stealing hours like a thief.

I reach out to it,
Its blackened hand dark.
But I can feel its touch,
And it leaves a mark.

It still holds on,
Pulling me apart.
It's like a cycle,
Going back to the start.

They gave me pills,
Then more on top,
And finally the dark,
Started to stop.

It can't rain all the time,
I lift up a shield.
I now see the light,
As the rain starts to yield.

I gather up my strength,
And ball up the light.
I push sunshine at the gloom.
I finally feel the fight.

The shadow retreats,
But I know it's always there.
So instead I give it love,
The little I can spare.

About the Author

Sabrina RG Raven is a writer and artist from Brisbane, Australia. She has been affected by mental illness for most of her life. Being creative has been her go to therapy through most of this time.

She wanted to write this book to give hope to those with mental health issues. Everyone's journey is different but never think you are alone.

To view more of Sabrina's art head to
www.sabrinargraven.com
Facebook and Instagram @sabrinargraven

For more info on her current books and future projects head to
www.ouroborusbooks.com

If you need help see your doctor or a list of world wide helplines can be found here
www.tinyurl.com/worldhelplines

www.ingramcontent.com/pod-product-compliance
Lightning Source LLC
Chambersburg PA
CBHW041714290426
44110CB00024B/2832